Rookie
Read-About® Science

Energy Is Everywhere

By June Young

Subject Consultant
Andrew Fraknoi
Chair, Astronomy Program
Foothill College
Los Altos Hills, California

Reading Consultant
Cecilia Minden-Cupp, PhD
Former Director of the Language and Literacy Program
Harvard Graduate School of Education
Cambridge, Massachusetts

Children's Press®
A Division of Scholastic Inc.
New York   Toronto   London   Auckland   Sydney
Mexico City   New Delhi   Hong Kong
Danbury, Connecticut

Designer: Herman Adler Design
Photo Researcher: Caroline Anderson
The photo on the cover shows a family roasting marshmallows over a campfire.

Library of Congress Cataloging-in-Publication Data

Young, June, 1954–
    Energy is everywhere / by June Young; consultants, Andrew Fraknoi,
Cecilia Minden-Cupp.
        p. cm. — (Rookie Read-About Science)
    Includes index.
    ISBN 0-516-25902-4 (lib. bdg.)   0-516-28003-1 (pbk.)
    1. Force and energy—Juvenile literature. 2. Matter—Juvenile literature.
I. Title. II. Series.
    QC73.4.Y68 2006
    531'.6—dc22   2005023922

CHILDREN'S PRESS, and ROOKIE READ-ABOUT®,
and associated logos are trademarks and/or registered trademarks
of Scholastic Library Publishing. SCHOLASTIC and associated logos
are trademarks and/or registered trademarks of Scholastic Inc.

1 2 3 4 5 6 7 8 9 10 R 15 14 13 12 11 10 09 08 07 06

Sometimes you feel it.
Sometimes you see it.
Sometimes you hear it.
Energy is everywhere.

Energy comes from matter. Matter is what things are made of.

Air. Sand. Water. People. Everything on a beach is made of matter.

Matter in the Sun gives off energy. It gives off energy you can feel with your skin. It gives off energy you can see with your eyes.

Wiggle your toes in the sand. Do you feel the heat?

The energy from the Sun makes the sand hot. Heat is energy.

9

10

Wear your sunglasses. Put on your sun visor. Sunlight is bright. Light is energy.

Children yell. Dogs bark.
Sound is energy, too.

14

The wind blows.
Waves splash.
Movement is also energy.

Find some wood.
Stack it tall. It's time
for a cookout.

Sizzle. Pop. The wood burns. It gives off sound energy you can hear.

Sizzle. Pop. The wood burns. It gives off light energy you can see.

Sizzle. Pop. The wood burns. It gives off heat energy you can feel.

Put the hot dogs on
the fire. Cook the
marshmallows, too.
Yum. Yum.

The food changes to
energy inside you.

Night has come. The air feels cold. Moonlight shines on the water. Waves whisper good night. It's time to go home.

Sometimes you feel it.
Sometimes you see it.
Sometimes you hear it.
Energy is everywhere.

Words You Know

cookout

heat energy

light energy

matter

moonlight

sound energy

Index

About the Author

June Young lives in Austin, Texas, where energy is all around her.

Photo Credits